WILLIAM STEIG

ALADDIN PAPERBACKS

New York London Toronto Sydney Singapore

For Charlotte Reine Steiner

First Aladdin Paperbacks edition May 2003

Copyright © 1968 by William Steig
Revised Format Edition, 2000

ALADDIN PAPERBACKS
An imprint of Simon & Schuster
Children's Publishing Division
1230 Avenue of the Americas
New York, NY 10020

Also available in a Simon & Schuster Books for Young Readers hardcover edition.
Designed by Jennifer Reyes
The text of this book was set in Avant Garde Bold ITC.
The illustrations were rendered in watercolors.

Manufactured in China
2 4 6 8 10 9 7 5 3 1

The Library of Congress has cataloged the hardcover edition as follows:
Steig, William, 1907-
CDB! / by William Steig.
p.   cm.
Summary: Letters and numbers are used to create the sounds of words and simple sentences
4 u 2 figure out with the aid of illustrations.
ISBN 0-689-83160-9 (hc.)
1. Word games—Juvenile literature. [1. Word games. 2. Games.] I. Title. II. Title: CDB!
GV1507.W8S75 2000 793.734—dc21 99-32720

ISBN 0-689-85706-3 (Aladdin pbk.)

C D B!

D B S A B-Z B.
O, S N-D!

I N-V U.

R U C-P?

S, I M.

I M 2.

A P-N-E 4 U.

K-T S
X-M-N-N
D N-6.

D N S 5 X.

I M 2 O-L 4 U.

O U Q-T.
U R A B-U-T.

I M B-4 U.

R U O-K?

S, N Q.

I M A U-M B-N.

U R N N-M-L.

D C-L S N D C.

D D-R S N D I-V.

D L-F-N 8 D A.

S E-Z 4 U. S?

B-4 U X-M-N L-C, X-M-N R-V.

H-U!

Y R U Y-N-N?

I N O.

I C U.

S N-E-1 N?

L-X-&-R N I

R N D C-T.

I N O.

K-T S D-Z.

I C Y.

I 8 U!

I 8 U 2!

F U R B-Z,
I-L 1 O-A.

E S D 1 4 U 2 C.

I M N D L-F-8-R.

M N X R L-T 4 U!

I M C-N A G-P-C.

N-R-E S N T-S.

I M N
A T-P.

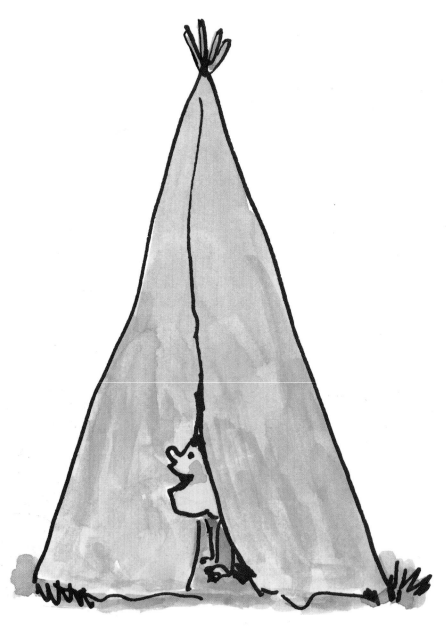

P-T N J R N J-L.

O 4 A 2-L.

E-R S A M-R.

S M-T!

I F-N
N-E
N-R-G.

I M C-N U!

N-D U R. U R P-K-N.

P-T S N N-M-E.

I O U 6 X.

O, I C M. N Q.

D Y-N S X-L-N!

O-L H.

I O U A J.

I M N N-D-N.

O, I C.

U 8 L D X!

L-C S N X-T-C.

Answer Key

Page 3   C D B! = See the bee!
       D B S A B-Z B. = The bee is a busy bee.
       0, S N-D! = Oh, yes indeed!

Page 4   I N-V U. = I envy you.

Page 5   R U C-P? = Are you sleepy?
       S, I M. = Yes, I am.
       I M 2. = I am too.

Page 6   A P-N-E 4 U. = A peony for you.

Page 7   K-T S X-M-N-N D N-6. = Katy is examining the insects.

Page 8   D N S 5 X. = The hen has five eggs.

Page 9   I M 2 O-L 4 U. = I am too old for you.

Page 10   O U Q-T. = Oh you cutie.
       U R A B-U-T. = You are a beauty.

Page 11   I M B-4 U. = I am before you.

Page 12   R U O-K? = Are you ok?
       S, N Q. = Yes, thank you.

Page 13   I M A U-M B-N. = I am a human being.
       U R N N-M-L. = You are an animal.

Page 14   D C-L S N D C. = The seal is in the sea.

Page 15   D D-R S N D I-V. = The deer is in the ivy.

Page 16   D L-F-N 8 D A. = The elephant ate the hay.

Page 17   S E-Z 4 U. S? = It's easy for you. Yes?

Page 18   B-4 U X-M-N L-C, = Before you examine Elsie,
       X-M-N R-V. = examine Harvey.

Page 19   H-U! = Achoo!

Page 20   Y R U Y-N-N? = Why are you whinin'?
       I N O. = I don't know.

Page 21   I C U. = I see you.

Page 22   S N-E-T N? = Is anyone in?

Page 23   L-X-&-R N I R N D C-T. = Alexander and I are in the city.

Page 24   I N O. = I don't know.

Page 25   K-T S D-Z. = Katy is dizzy.
       I C Y. = I see why.

Page 26   I 8 U! = I hate you!
       I 8 U 2! = I hate you too!

Page 27   F U R B-Z, = If you are busy,
       I-L 1 O-A. = I'll run away.

Page 29   E S D 1 4 U 2 C. = He is the one for you to see.

Page 30   I M N D L-F-8-R. = I am in the elevator.

Page 31   M N X R L-T 4 U! = Ham and eggs are healthy for you!

Page 32   I M C-N A G-P-C. = I am seeing a gypsy.

Page 33   N-R-E S N T-S. = Henry is in tears.

Page 34   I M N A T-P. = I am in a teepee.

Page 35   P-T N J-R N J-L. = Petey and Jay are in jail.

Page 36   O 4 A 2-L. = Oh, for a tool.
       E-R S A M-R. = Here is a hammer.

Page 37   S M-T! = It's empty!

Page 38   I F-N N-E N-R-G. = I haven't any energy.

Page 39   I M C-N U! = I am seeing you!
       N-D U R U R P-K-N. = Indeed you are. You are peeking.

Page 40   P-T S N N-M-E. = Petey has an enemy.

Page 41   I O U 6 X. = I owe you six eggs.
       O, I C M. N Q. = Oh, I see them. Thank you.

Page 42   D Y-N S X-L-N! = The wine is excellent!

Page 43   O-L H. = Old age.

Page 44   I O U A J. = I owe you a jay.

Page 45   I M N N-D-N. = I am an Indian.
       O, I C. = Oh, I see.

Page 46   U 8 L D X! = You ate all the eggs!

Page 47   L-C S N X-T-C. = Elsie is in ecstasy.